10% Thoughts for 90% Life

Master a Positive Mindset

LAKSHMI SAGAR G

DEDICATION

The book **"10% Thoughts for 90% Life"** is dedicated to all the readers. I personally thank my parents, my teachers, my brother, my close ones, and my friends.

Copyright

Preface

The title of this book may make you think about which 10 % of thoughts can make us 90% better life. Look at the difference between poor and rich, intelligent and idiot, successful and unsuccessful. We can observe a common trend: trust in their positive thinking and belief in their action. "Whether you think you can or think you can't, you're probably right" is a quote by Henry Ford. This book gives 10 key points to improve your positive mindset. The book is quick and straight to the point on every page, not wasting much time. Every line in this book is constructed to raise positive thinking in readers' minds. The topics include learning, aim, focus, stress, pressure, productivity, self-doubt, motivation, procrastination, starting early, and enjoying a happy life. The book is written in simple language to convey all these self-help messages to readers.

The author has blogging experience in short motivational articles. This book is his seventh book. He writes on work motivation, goal setting, productivity, overcoming procrastination, overcoming failures, and achieving dreams. Most people love his articles on Reddit. He aims to motivate people to build a happy and successful life. His more than one lakh ebooks sold out on platforms like Google Playbook and Amazon, with thousands of positive reviews from readers.

If you are struggling with a lack of confidence, then this book is strongly dedicated to you.

Welcome,

Unlock Your Success.

CONTENTS

"It is during our darkest moments that we must focus to see the light."

- Aristotle Onassis

Start With a Good Morning

The time we wake up and what we think in the early morning is significant. That's the time when we initiate the reaction of thoughts. You have a few minutes to decide your day. Plough new positive thoughts every day. Don't give up on this process because negative thoughts also don't give up. They come to you every day with even more vital. Don't be a victim of those. To defeat those, we must achieve our inner strength. You cannot erase the past but replace it with a better future. Forget about your yesterday and focus on how to make your today productive and joyful.

Why do we only think that a selfish world exists every minute?

If this also exists, then the opposite to this must exist. If people hate you for no reason, you also find people who love you without reason. You will find people who can understand you.

Why fill our minds with toxic thoughts? And what's the use?

Come out from those. Repair your thoughts because you are living for yourself, and at least give yourself what you deserve. You should not leave every day with toxic thoughts. There is a heaven outside of it waiting for you.

Don't forget to smile. Practice to smile and practice to love. One thing that will always multiply by giving it to others is love. I am not only talking about love between humans but also between humans and animals, between humans and plants, and between humans and nature. We all experienced this and believe this feeling is heaven on this earth.

Isn't that so?

When you wake up early in the morning, Go into nature and close your eyes. Breathe fresh air and feel the beauty of your inner world.

Feel the presence of God, and feel his blessing for you.

Tell yourself, "I love this world, I love people around me, I love myself, I love my smile, and I believe in that. With my smile, I only initiate my surroundings; I know this will test my patience, but it will create a healthy atmosphere for me, and I will try my best."

"Don't give more chances for negative thoughts. Before they occupy, fill your mind with positivity."

"Anyone who stops learning is old, whether at twenty or eighty. Anyone who keeps learning stays young. The greatest thing in life is to keep your mind young."

-Henry Ford

Learning is a Key

Working for your goals is not easy. Every time, it will test your patience. Maybe sometimes you will find no hope. You will be forced to give up. Perhaps you are stuck in a cycle of confusion, And you feel like all your efforts have been wasted. Still, you may be in the way of finding your perfection.

When you think you achieved perfection, it will be hard for you to accept reality. Good is the best. It will be even harder to take when you compare yourself to others. After some time, it realizes that comparison is our enemy. I know it isn't easy to move on, I know it isn't easy to admit it, and I know it isn't easy to work again on it.

But believe in learning because that is the only hook that will help you to rise. Trust me, the deeper you fall, the better you rise, but what you learn from that fall matters. Don't worry; confusion later itself joins perfection.

Apply **Ant's principle**, 'Start again from zero, start again from zero, and then start again from zero.' Think like a beginner once again and realize there is much to learn. Give attention to the step you slipped, work on it again, and return like a master.

"Work for what you are worth every time, not what you want. As long as you are eager to learn, you will not accept the defeat."

"Your work is going to fill a large part of your life, and the only way to be truly satisfied is to do what you believe is great work. And the only way to do great work is to love what you do. If you haven't found it yet, keep looking. Don't settle. As with all matters of the heart, you'll know when you find it."

- Steve Jobs

Enjoying Now is Enjoying Life

Think about the work you did without any breaks. We can't do this for many hours. We will be tired. This tiredness is enough to ruin our energy. It is, moreover, a mental issue. This tiredness is nothing, but we are not enjoying it. Enjoying the work brings happiness, and struggling in the work brings tiredness. This stress will convert to significant diseases after some time.

How much stress can anybody take in a day?

We don't have an exact answer for this. It will vary from person to person, situation to situation, and many more aspects.

Do this exercise: hold a 5 kg bag for a few minutes. At first, it may feel light, but when you have it for a long time, you will realize the stress it creates on your muscles.

The longer we hold anything, the heavier it feels for us. It applies to every aspect of life. Our mind is also designed like this: a small break can refill energy. Switching to other work is also refreshing, but switching and multitasking differ. Multitasking is about doing various tasks at a time. For example, writing with both hands, reading a book while listening to music, and many more. It requires a very high level of concentration, which is not easy for everyone.

Switching may feel easy because we concentrate on different things at different times. It keeps us busy throughout the day and avoids the boredom of doing a single task. In this process, we define what is important to us, and in our free time, we enjoy doing other tasks to fill our motivation bar. By enjoying every action, we can avoid stress, anxiety, depression, and other problems as well.

You may work intense 8 hours a day, but an hour walk in the park can reduce your stress level and increase your energy. Observe this when you think for a long time;

you may not find the solution, but that solution may pop up in your mind in a relaxing mood.

Maybe that's the reason for the kid's happiness. Children don't even know how to stick to a single task. If they find it boring, then they will switch to other activities where they can find happiness.

I used to think, what may be the reason behind their energy?

How do children feel such energy throughout the day?

Later, I found that we will not get life experience in one single task, but it is all about knowledge accumulated of different actions we perform.

For example, when a person succeeds in learning football, that knowledge applies to playing football and every aspect of life. He may learn to coordinate with people around him, figure out the best thing for him, and find courage in his actions. We can apply our experience to any other task if applicable.

This type of switching can build self-confidence in us. Sometimes, being off the track is also beneficial. But we must not forget what is essential and use our spare time for things we love.

A piece of relaxing music, a few minutes of meditation, playing some sports, a simple walk in the greenery, enjoying the dance steps we know, one good habit you like, spending a healthy time with family, and many more can boost our productivity to the next level.

It is impossible to do nothing because we will do something every minute. Even if it may relax or other things, our minds will be busy every minute.

Switching is naturally present in us, but we may have lost it somewhere in our busy lives. This energy will always motivate us to explore life even better. It is time now to regain what we lost.

"It is better to find time to engage with what we enjoy."

"Opportunities don't happen. You create them."

- Chris Grosser

Motivation to Work

After being knocked down, we have to think even more about it. However, I observed that some people will tap out during difficult times and suffer. I tell you, it is not that easy. If it is easy, then anybody can achieve it. It is like a puzzle; keep yourself calm, and it has only one exit door. Nobody will clear this in one shot. Try to find your way and try to find that exit. Just move on.

At least daily, think about your goals and do not feel it wastes time because your thinking only leads to your actions.

Try to think, and try to think about it even more.

How many days do you think about your goals?

At least at some point, you will start to work on them. Only desires can reach you for your destination. Design your destination. Your journey and efforts are yours; nobody can take this from you.

No one is born with built-in skills, but I agree that some people will learn things quickly. However, that learning can happen at any stage of life, and it may be from this minute. It is not late yet. You can achieve anything in life but try to focus on basic skills.

I know that working for many may not work for you, but that knowledge will give you a new style of doing things. Try to do that as no other person can do it as beautiful as you. That is the power within you.

It may be your kind words, it may be your craft, it may be your purest feelings, or it may be your burning desire to achieve something.

"Never think it's too late. Today is a better day than any other day. If not today, don't think of another day that doesn't exist."

"The people who are crazy enough to think they can change the world are the ones who do."

– Steve Jobs

Self-doubt is Culprit

How to know? I am better at what I am doing.
How can I measure my efforts?
Whether I am not taking it the wrong way?

Some self-doubt will lift us to another level.
But there should be a limitation for everything.

Find a balanced way, and everything will run
smoothly in this way. If there is a problem,
there must also be a solution.

Do you know? Where are you able to
reach? Where are you not?
What is your strength? Where do you fail?

Is there any chance to overcome that failure?
If you see possibilities to win in this situation,
what's wrong with taking chances?

These questions will only give you the right way to go ahead. These are all your imagination; they help you start, but the real test is for your efforts.

It's all about predicting what it needs. If you do not act, things will become even more challenging to solve.

Believe in what you are doing. You are showing the world that this is your approach. It is another way to get it done. You should be ready to put your heart and soul into it. Don't worry; if you analyzed it correctly, believed it strongly, doing everything correctly, then how would you go wrong? Fill courage in your mind, do the right things, and believe in them.

Think about what needs to be done, when, and what needs to be done. It will get done.

"If you doubt yourself in what you are doing, you can not do what you want to do. Belief is like a sword. It works great when it is sharp."

"Nothing in life is to be feared, it is only to be understood. Now is the time to understand more, so that we may fear less."

— Marie Curie

Handling Stress and Pressure

Failures make us weak. We feel we are helpless and hopeless. You dreamed something, and you invested yourself in that. Try to lift yourself. One success may be a result of a hundred failures. Don't fear failing. That means you are ready to overcome them. Get up and train yourself to beat failures.

Thinking all the time about failures will not do any favors. Sometimes, it seems impossible to overcome those, and actions to overcome them can make us tired.

Pressure creates two persons: one is a victim, and the other is a winner. Yes, I am talking about positive pressure.

It's all about how we take that pressure and welcome it. It can change the whole scenario for you. Stress is the result of avoiding those pressures. You can see wonders in your life if you welcome pressure with a calm mind. Changing your thoughts can change everything for you.

Say to yourself, " <u>This pressure came today to lift me, enlighten me, make me even stronger, teach me something different, and open me to higher opportunities.</u>"

Wrong keys will not open the right door for you. Have patience; a fresh mind can do magical things for you.

Daily, you will make new patterns in your mind, slowly reaching the actual pattern to open that door. It will take some time.

Try to work with your heart and show your highest devotion. Analyze what it needs and where you are failing. Make yourself strong in every little aspect of your work. Believe that things will change because when they change, you will see the strongest warrior coming out of that situation. That's you.

"Wrong keys will not open the right door for you. Have patience; a fresh mind can do magical things for you."

"You were born to win, but to be a winner, you must plan to win, prepare to win, and expect to win."

-Zig Ziglar

Finding an Easy Way

If a person experiences many failures, then think about his confidence level. Compare his energy level to when he started; you will find a significant difference. His mindset will be weak; instead of finding the answer, he will question his abilities now. But this is not his dark side, and it is not wrong to think like this. Yes, he fell without knowing the ups and downs, but now he knows a few things about that path. This experience made him firm, and now he has learned how to think and analyze situations.

It is a great lesson to stand up for failures. But in this stage, one of the obstacles to our growth will be our narrow thinking.

Our thinking may be broad as a beginner, but it was focusless. As experienced people, our thinking should be even broader with laser focus intensity. However, the negative part is that we close our mind's possibilities to think narrowly. Don't make your experience an obstacle to your success. It is sometimes easy to win, but our past experiences open us to a difficult path. A nail cutter will never do the work of the ax, and an ax will never do the work of the nail cutter. We have to choose our tools wisely before working on something. Our 50% victory depends on our tool; that is how we think of solutions for our problems.

When I was learning table tennis, I didn't even know how to play it as a beginner. I was giving my attention to the ball by holding my hands tight, but I failed to hit that ball every time.

My friend observed this, and he said, "Make your body free and play with a calm mind; then automatically, your hands will play."

Yes, it was true. Sometimes our minds will be filled with complex thoughts, but even we try to go with that. It is better to make big decisions with a calm mind. Don't stress yourself; it will decrease your confidence. Don't block your body, and don't even blank your mind. Even in tough times, believe in yourself and your abilities. Tell yourself constantly, "I can do this." Indeed, it will open you to an easy path to do that.

"A good player will never make his game difficult; instead, he finds every chance to make it as easy as possible."

"And, when you want something, all the universe conspires in helping you to achieve it."

— Paulo Coelho, The Alchemist

Focus Properly

You may have a fear about your performance. You may have fears about your future and many more. These fears are natural, and sometimes, they are helpful. If we don't have fear, imagining our life is very difficult. Because many fears make us secure in our lives, don't you think so? Fear of falling prevented us from falling. Pain makes us even more potent. The small hurdles we face today will prepare us for the upcoming big ones. These positive things will make us productive and better every time. The situation will not bring us joy or sorrow, but our choice towards that situation will decide the outcome.

It depends on that; how do we take those situations?

What is the perspective of us?

The teacher teaches the same for all, but few people will be successful because they grasp it correctly. So, how we react to every situation matters a lot.

Karate master saw a newly joined kid suffering to learn the kicks. That kid wants to be best at every kick. But he was crying, complaining that he was not perfect at all those kicks.

Master appreciated that kid's devotion and told him, "Kid, you may have 99 weaknesses, but focus on one strength you have. Practice that one kick; no one can hit that better than you. Trust me, one day, that one strength will dominate all those your 99 weaknesses".

It is not different from life as well. Those willing to solve this puzzle will go to the next level. Suffering is a path that takes us away from the solution. Sit with a peaceful mind and try to see the mistake. You will probably get a solution and even don't suffer for things that are not in your hands.

"It is better to focus on what we are capable of because we already know something about it."

"I insist on a lot of time being spent, almost every day, to just sit and think. That is very uncommon in American business. I read and think. So I do more reading and thinking, and make less impulse decisions than most people in business. I do it because I like this kind of life."

- Warren Buffett

Aim What You Want

You may be thinking about your dreams daily. Every day, you try hard to move closer to your dreams. It isn't easy to believe that we will achieve all of those. Many times, you may ask yourself, "Is this possible?"

But I suggest you look back on your journey. One day, you may have thought reaching here was also impossible, but congrats, you are here. It would not be possible without your courage. Most importantly, we aimed one day to be here. That's great, and that's how we are here. To execute our plans, we must work with the aim. Aim helps us to focus on a single direction. Only focus can control our stress; focus can help us achieve more in less time, and focus is like meditation. We all wish to be in this state of mind, but one distraction is enough to ruin our valuable hours. To avoid this, we must know where we are going. We must know whether this path is taking us towards or away from our dreams. It is impossible to reach that place without knowing where we are going.

We must question ourselves daily, "Where are we going?" and "What is our destination?"

Note down every day how many hours you are giving for your dreams. Question yourself: Are they worth it, or do they deserve more?

The only particular key will open a specific lock because of its pattern. With the help of focus, unlock your problems with your thinking patterns. It is expected to be distracted, but make your mind focus on your aim repeatedly. But I am not suggesting you make yourself tired in this process. You should enjoy your day, and you should do your duty as well. At the same time, you must be productive. I know making this habit will consume more time. Trust me, when we know them, it will be easier for us. You will achieve the 'flow state' and feel it interesting.

"Remember, interest comes from focus; there is nothing called boring. If we feel so, then we are not focusing on it."

"You must be very patient, very persistent. The world isn't going to shower gold coins on you just because you have a good idea. You're going to have to work like crazy to bring that idea to the attention of people."

- Herb Kelleher

Productivity Formula

You plan something, and you may fail to execute it. You have time. You have energy, and you have everything to do that work. Still, you shift it to some other day. It is the complaint of many.

Now, guess! What is the reason for that?

Being productive is not one-time work, and it should be cultivated every day to be efficient in what we are doing.

You did everything right, but you forgot to give one push to it. To enjoy the playground slide, you must make one push.

Anything that you do not push will not happen. Push up to some point from your side, and things will push your work to the end.

Getting up early in the morning requires some thoughts at night, which needs your push. And when you wake up, you must push yourself a little to win your day. That positive push makes you aware, but it will not burn you.

If you are struggling within yourself to do anything, then remember it all needs some push. Make it now, and things will take off.

Yeah, this is hard in the beginning. But doing easy things will not bring you a win, and it is not always hard for you.

Win your day by giving a little bit more energy at the beginning. Yes, it makes us uncomfortable sometimes. But it will reach us to the top of our work. Let's make that positive push.

"To enjoy the playground slide, you must make one push."

Check Out Other Books by Author

- ✓ If you like this book, follow author for future updates.
- ✓ Please share this with your loved ones.
- ✓ Please give your honest review for this book and encourage the readership.
- ✓ Don't forget to checkout other self help books by the author.

Thank You

www.ingramcontent.com/pod-product-compliance
Lightning Source LLC
Chambersburg PA
CBHW032001140726
47988CB00019B/3076